D1440729

Bronze

Bronze

A Book of Verse

Georgia Douglas Johnson

MINT EDITIONS

Bronze: A Book of Verse was first published in 1922.

This edition published by Mint Editions 2021.

ISBN 9781513209241 | E-ISBN 9781513293547

Published by Mint Editions®

 MINT
EDITIONS

minteditionbooks.com

Publishing Director: Jennifer Newens
Design & Production: Rachel Lopez Metzger
Project Manager: Micaela Clark
Typesetting: Westchester Publishing Services

Contents

Foreword by W.E.B. DuBois

Those who know what it means to be a colored woman in 1922—and know it not so much in fact as in feeling, apprehension, unrest and delicate yet stern thought—must read Georgia Douglas Johnson's Bronze. Much of it will not touch this reader and that, and some of it will mystify and puzzle them as a sort of reiteration and over-emphasis. But none can fail to be caught here and there by a word—a phrase—a period that tells a life history or even paints the history of a generation. Can you not see that marching of the mantled with

"Voices strange to ecstasy?"

Have you ever looked on the "twilight faces" of their throngs, or seen the black mother with her son when

"Her heart is sandaling his feet?"

Or can you not conceive that infinite sorrow of a dark child wandering the world:

"Seeking the breast of an unknown face!"

I hope Mrs. Johnson will have wide reading. Her word is simple, sometimes trite, but it is singularly sincere and true, and as a revelation of the soul struggle of the women of a race it is invaluable.

W. E. B. Du Bois
New York, August 4, 1922

Author's Note

This book is the child of a bitter earth-wound. I sit on the earth and sing—sing out, and of, my sorrow. Yet, fully conscious of the potent agencies that silently work in their healing ministries, I know that God's sun shall one day shine upon a perfected and unhampered people.

EXHORTATION

Sonnet to the Mantled

And they shall rise and cast their mantles by,
Erect and strong and visioned, in the day
That rings the knell of Curfew o'er the sway
Of prejudice—who reels with mortal cry
To lift no more her leprous, blinded eye.
Reft of the fetters, far more cursed than they
Which held dominion o'er human clay.
The spirit soars aloft where rainbows lie.

Like joyful exiles swift returning home—
The rhythmic chanson of their eager feet.
While voices strange to ecstasy, long dumb.
Break forth in major rhapsodies, full sweet.
Into the very star-shine, lo! they come
Wearing the bays of victory complete!

SONNET TO THOSE WHO SEE BUT DARKLY

Their gaze uplifting from shoals of despair
Like phantoms groping enswathed from the light
Up from miasmic depths, children of night,
Surge to the piping of Hope's dulcet lay,
Souled like the lily, whose splendors declare
God's mazèd paradox—purged of all blight.
Out from the quagmire, unsullied and fair.

Life holds her arms o'er the festering way,
Smiles, as their faith-sandalled rushes prevail,
Slowly the sun rides the marge of the day.
Wine to the lips sorely anguished and pale;
On, ever on, do the serried ranks sway
Charging the ultimate, rending the veil.

BROTHERHOOD

Come, brothers all!
Shall we not wend
The blind-way of our prison-world
By sympathy entwined?
Shall we not make
The bleak way for each other's sake
Less rugged and unkind?
O let each throbbing heart repeat
The faint note of another's beat
To lift a chanson for the feet
That stumble down life's checkered street.

SUPPLICATION

LET ME NOT LOSE MY DREAM

Let me not lose my dream, e'en though I scan the veil with eyes
    unseeing through their glaze of tears,
Let me not falter, though the rungs of fortune perish as I fare above
    the tumult, praying purer air,
Let me not lose the vision, gird me. Powers that toss the worlds,
    I pray!
Hold me, and guard, lest anguish tear my dreams away!

Let Me Not Hate

Let me not hate, although the bruising world decries my peace,
Gives me no quarter, hounds me while I sleep;
Would snuff the candles of my soul and sear my inmost dreamings.
Let me not hate, though girt by vipers, green and hissing through the
    dark;
I fain must love. God help me keep the altar-gleams that flicker
    wearily, anon,
On down the world's grim night!

GEORGIA DOUGLAS JOHNSON

CALLING DREAMS

The right to make my dreams come true
I ask, nay, I demand of life,
Nor shall fate's deadly contraband
Impede my steps, nor countermand.
Too long my heart against the ground
Has beat the dusty years around,
And now, at length, I rise, I wake!
And stride into the morning-break!

Desire

Ope! ye everlasting doors, unto my soul's demand,
I would go forward, fare beyond these dusty boulevards,
Faint lights and fair allure me all insistently
And I must stand within the halls resplendent, of my dreams.

SHADOW

SORROW SINGERS

Hear their viol-voices ringing
Down the corridor of years,
As they lift their twilight faces
Through a mist of falling tears!

THE CROSS

All day the world's mad mocking strife,
The venomed prick of probing knife,
The baleful, subtle leer of scorn
That rims the world from morn to morn,
While reptile-visions writhe and creep
Into the very arms of sleep
To quench the fitful burnished gleams:
A crucifixion in my dreams!

Prejudice

These fell miasmic rings of mist, with ghoulish menace bound,
Like noose-horizons tightening my little world around,
They still the soaring will to wing, to dance, to speed away.
And fling the soul insurgent back into its shell of clay:

Beneath incrusted silences, a seething Etna lies.
The fire of whose furnaces may sleep—*but never dies!*

LAOCOÖN

This spirit-choking atmosphere
    With deadly serpent-coil
Entwines my soaring-upwardness
    And chains me to the soil,
Where'er I seek with eager stride
    To gain yon gleaming height,
These noisesome fetters coil aloft
    And snare my buoyant flight.

O, why these aspirations bold,
    These rigours of desire.
That surge within so ceaselessly
    Like living tongues of fire?
And why these glowing forms of hope
    That scintillate and shine,
If naught of all that burnished dream
    Can evermore be mine?
It cannot be, fate does not mock,
    And man's untoward decree
Shall not forever thus confine
    My life's entirety,
My every fibre fierce rebels
    Against this servile role,
And all my being broods to break
    This death-grip from my soul!

Moods

My heart is pregnant with a great despair
With much beholding of my people's care,
'Mid blinded prejudice and nurtured wrong,
Exhaling wantonly the days along:
I mark Faith's fragile craft of cheering light
Tossing imperiled on the sea of night,
And then, enanguished, comes my heart's low cry,
"God, God! I crave to learn the reason why!"
Again, in spirit loftily I soar
With winged vision through earth's outer door.
In such an hour, it is mine to see,
In frowning fortune smiling destiny!

The Hegira

Oh, black man, why do you northward roam, and leave all the farm lands
bare?
Is your house not warm, tightly thatched from storm, and a larder replete
your share?
And have you not schools, fit with books and tools the steps of your young
to guide?
Then what do you seek, in the north cold and bleak, 'mid the whirl
of its teeming tide?

I have toiled in your cornfields, and parched in the sun,
    I have bowed 'neath your load of care,
I have patiently garnered your bright golden grain, in season of storm
    and fair.
With a smile I have answered your glowering gloom, while my
    wounded heart quivering bled.
Trailing mute in your wake, as your rosy dawn breaks, while I curtain
    the mound of my dead.

Though my children are taught in the schools you have wrought, they
    are blind to the sheen of the sky,
For the brand of your hand, casts a pall o'er the land, that enshadows
    the gleam of the eye.
My sons, deftly sapped of the brawn-hood of man, self-rejected and
    impotent stand,
My daughters, unhaloed, unhonored, undone, feed the lust of a
    dominant land.

I would not remember, yet could not forget, how the hearts beating
    true to your own.
You've tortured, and wounded, and filtered their blood 'till a budding
    Hegira has blown.

Unstrange is the pathway to Calvary's hill, which I wend in my dumb
    agony,
Up its perilous height, in the pale morning light, to dissever my own
    from the tree.

And so I'm away, where the sky-line of day sets the arch of its rainbow
    afar,
To the land of the north, where the symbol of worth sets the broad
    gates of combat ajar!

The Passing of the Ex-Slave

Swift melting into yesterday,
The tortured hordes of ebon-clay;
No more is heard the plaintive strain,
The rhythmic chaunting of their pain.

Their mounded bodies dimly rise
To fill the gulf of sacrifice,
And o'er their silent hearts below
The mantled millions softly go.

Some few remaining still abide.
Gnarled sentinels of time and tide.
Now mellowed by a chastened glow
Which lighter hearts will never know.

Winding into the silent way,
Spent with the travail of the day,
So royal in their humble might
These uncrowned Pilgrims of the Night!

GEORGIA DOUGLAS JOHNSON

THE OCTOROON

One drop of midnight in the dawn of life's pulsating stream
Marks her an alien from her kind, a shade amid its gleam;
Forevermore her step she bends insular, strange, apart—
And none can read the riddle of her wildly warring heart.

The stormy current of her blood beats like a mighty sea
Against the man-wrought iron bars of her captivity.
For refuge, succor, peace and rest, she seeks that humble fold
Whose every breath is kindliness, whose hearts are purest gold.

ALIENS

(To You—Everywhere! Dedicated)

They seem to smile as others smile, the masquerader's art
Conceals them, while, in verity, they're eating out their heart.
Betwixt the two contending stones of crass humanity
They lie, the fretted fabric of a dual dynasty.

A single drop, a sable strain debars them from their own,—
The others—fold them furtively, but God! they are alone.
Blown by the fickle winds of fate far from the traveled mart
To die, when they have quite consumed the morsel of their heart.
When man shall lift his lowered eyes to meet the moon of truth,
Shall break the shallow shell of pride and wax in ways of ruth,
He cannot hate, for love shall reign untrammelled in the soul,
While peace shall spread a rainbow o'er the earth from pole to pole.

GEORGIA DOUGLAS JOHNSON

Concord

Nor shall I in sorrow repine,
But offer a paean of praise
To the infinite God of my days
Who marshals the pivoting spheres
Through the intricate maze of the years,
Who loosens the luminous flood
That lightens the purlieus of men,
I shall not in sorrow repine
To break the eternal Amen!

MOTHERHOOD

THE MOTHER

The mother soothes her mantled child
With incantation sad and wild;
A deep compassion brims her eye
And stills upon her lips, the sigh.

Her thoughts are leaping down the years,
O'er branding bars, through seething tears,
Her heart is sandaling his feet
Adown the world's corroding street.

Then, with a start she dons a smile
His tender yearnings to beguile.
And only God will ever know
The wordless measure of her woe.

Maternity

Proud?
Perhaps—and yet
I cannot say with surety
That I am happy thus to be
Responsible for this young life's embarking.
Is he not thrall to prevalent conditions?
Does not the day loom dark apace
To weave its cordon of disgrace
Around his lifted throat?
Is not this mezzotint enough and surfeit
For such prescience?
Ah, did I dare
Recall the pulsing life I gave,
And fold him in the kindly grave!

Proud?
Perhaps—could I but ever so faintly scan
The broad horizon of a man
Swept fair for his dominion—
So hesitant and half-afraid
I view this babe of sorrow!

BLACK WOMAN*

Don't knock at my door, little child,
    I cannot let you in.
You know not what a world this is
    Of cruelty and sin.
Wait in the still eternity
    Until I come to you,
The world is cruel, cruel, child,
    I cannot let you in!

Don't knock at my heart, little one,
    I cannot bear the pain
Of turning deaf-ear to your call
    Time and time again!
You do not know the monster men
    Inhabiting the earth.
Be still, be still, my precious child,
    I must not give you birth!

* This poem was originally published as "Motherhood" in *The Crisis*.

"One of the Least of These, My Little One"

The infant eyes look out amazed upon the frowning earth,
A stranger, in a land now strange, child of the mantled-birth;
Waxing, he wonders more and more; the scowling grows apace;
A world, behind its barring doors, reviles his ebon face:

Yet from this maelstrom issues forth a God-like entity.
That loves a world all loveless, and smiles on Calvary!

GEORGIA DOUGLAS JOHNSON

SHALL I SAY, "MY SON, YOU'RE BRANDED?"*

Shall I say, "My son, you're branded in this country's pageantry,
By strange subtleties you're tethered, and no forum sets you free?"
Shall I mark the young lights fading through your
    soul-enchannelled eye,
As the dusky pall of shadows screen the highway of your sky?

Or shall I, with love prophetic, bid you dauntlessly arise.
Spurn the handicap that clogs you, taking what the world denies,
Bid you storm the sullen fortress wrought by prejudice and wrong
With a faith that shall not falter, in your heart and on your tongue!

---

* First published in *The Crisis*, August 1919.

My Boy

I hear you singing happily,
    My boy of tarnished mien,
Lifting your limpid, trustful gaze
    In innocence serene.

A thousand javelins of pain
    Assault my heaving breast
When I behold the storm of years
    That beat without your nest.

O sing, my lark, your matin song
    Of joyous rhapsody,
Distil the sweetness of the hours
    In gladsome ecstasy.

For time awaits your buoyant flight
    Across the bar of years.
Sing, sing your song, my bonny lark,
    Before it melts in tears!

GEORGIA DOUGLAS JOHNSON

GUARDIANSHIP

That dusky child upon your knee
Is breath of God's eternity;
Direct his vision to the height—
Let naught obscure his royal right.

Although the highways to renown
Are iron-barred by fortune's frown,
'Tis his to forge the master-key
That wields the locks of destiny!

Utopia

God grant you wider vision, clearer skies, my son,
With morning's rosy kisses on your brow;
May your wild yearnings know repose,
And storm-clouds break to smiles
As you sweep on with spreading wings
Unto a waiting sunset!

LITTLE SON

The very acme of my woe,
    The pivot of my pride,
My consolation, and my hope
    Deferred, but not denied.
The substance of my every dream,
    The riddle of my plight,
The very world epitomized
    In turmoil and delight.

BENEDICTION

Go forth, my son,
Winged by my heart's desire!
Great reaches, yet unknown,
Await
For your possession.
I may not, if I would.
Retrace the way with you,
My pilgrimage is through,
But life is calling you!
Fare high and far, my son,
A new day has begun.
Thy star-ways must be won!

GEORGIA DOUGLAS JOHNSON

PRESCIENCE

CREDO

I believe in the ultimate justice of Fate;
That the races of men front the sun in their turn;
That each soul holds the title to infinite wealth
In fee to the will as it masters itself;
That the heart of humanity sounds the same tone
In impious jungle, or sky-kneeling fane.
I believe that the key to the life-mystery
Lies deeper than reason and further than death.
I believe that the rhythmical conscience within
Is guidance enough for the conduct of men.

PROMISE

Through the moil and the gloom they have issued
    To the steps of the upwinding hill,
Where the sweet, dulcet pipes of tomorrow
    In their preluding rhapsodies trill.

With a thud comes a stir in the bosom,
    As there steals on the sight from afar,
Through a break of a cloud's coiling shadow
    The gleam of a bright morning star!

GEORGIA DOUGLAS JOHNSON

The Suppliant

Long have I beat with timid hands upon life's leaden door,
Praying the patient, futile prayer my fathers prayed before,
Yet I remain without the close, unheeded and unheard,
And never to my listening ear is borne the waited word.

Soft o'er the threshold of the years there comes this counsel cool:
The strong demand, contend, prevail; the beggar is a fool!

Hope

Frail children of sorrow, dethroned by a hue,
The shadows are flecked by the rose sifting through,
The world has its motion, all things pass away.
No night is omnipotent, there must be day.

The oak tarries long in the depth of the seed,
But swift is the season of nettle and weed.
Abide yet awhile in the mellowing shade.
And rise with the hour for which you were made.

The cycle of seasons, the tidals of man
Revolve in the orb of an infinite plan.
We move to the rhythm of ages long done,
And each has his hour—to dwell in the sun!

EXALTATION

COSMOPOLITE

Not wholly this or that,
But wrought
Of alien bloods am I,
A product of the interplay
Of traveled hearts.
Estranged, yet not estranged, I stand
All comprehending;
From my estate
I view earth's frail dilemma;
Scion of fused strength am I,
All understanding,
Nor this nor that
Contains me.

Fusion

How deftly does the gardener blend
This rose and that
To bud a new creation,
More gorgeous and more beautiful
Than any parent portion,
And so,
I trace within my warring blood
The tributary sources,
They potently commingle
And sweep
With new-born forces!

PERSPECTIVE

Some day
I shall be glad that it was mine to be
A dark fore-runner of a race burgeoning;
I then shall know
The secret of life's Calvary,
And bless the thorns
That wound me!

WHEN I RISE UP

When I rise above the earth,
And look down on the things that fetter me,
I beat my wings upon the air.
Or tranquil lie,
Surge after surge of potent strength
Like incense comes to me
When I rise up above the earth
And look down upon the things that fetter me.

GEORGIA DOUGLAS JOHNSON

FAITH

The faint lose faith
When in the tomb their all is laid,
And there returns
No echoing of weal or woe.
The strong hope on,
They see the clods close over head,
The grass grow green.
No word is said.
And yet—
A little world within the world
Are we,
Daily our hearts' high yearnings fade,
Are buried!
New ones are made,—
Are crucified!
And yet—

MARTIAL

We Face the Future

The hour is big with sooth and sign, with errant men at war,
While blood of alien, friend, and foe imbues the land afar,
And we, with sable faces pent, move with the vanguard line.
Shod with a faith that Springtime keeps, and all the stars opine.

SOLDIER

Though I should weep until the judgment,
How would it serve—
Brave men are fighting, women speed them,
'Tis a day
Of crucial conflict!
My son, sometimes it seems I'd rather hold
You safe beneath my heart
Than send you forth!
But lo! The sun is red and weaker children go!
Though I should weep until the judgment.
How would it serve!
I'll close my eyes and smile, O Son of Mine,
Your cause is kingly!
Step proud and confident, worthy your mother;
Be firm and brave, O Son of Mine, be strong.
For terror waxeth,
Speed swift away.
Though I should weep until the judgment. . .

GEORGIA DOUGLAS JOHNSON

Homing Braves

There's music in the measured tread
Of those returning from the dead
Like scattered flowers from a plain
So lately crimson, with the slain.

No more the sound of shuffled feet
Shall mark the poltroon on the street,
Nor shifting, sodden, downcast eye
Reveal the man afraid to die.

They shall have paid full, utterly
The price of peace across the sea,
When, with uplifted glance, they come
To claim a kindly welcome home.

Nor shall the old-time daedal sting
Of prejudice, their manhood wing.
Nor heights, nor depths, nor living streams
Stand in the pathway of their dreams!

Taps

They are embosomed in the sod,
In still and tranquil leisure,
Their lives they've cast like trifles down,
To serve their country's pleasure.

Nor bugle call, nor mother's voice.
Nor moody mob's unreason,
Shall break their solace and repose
Through swiftly changing season.

O graves of men who lived and died
Afar from life's high pleasures,
Fold them in tenderly and warm
With manifold fond measures.

GEORGIA DOUGLAS JOHNSON

PEACE

Peace on a thousand hills and dales,
Peace in the hearts of men
While kindliness reclaims the soil
Where bitterness has been.

The night of strife is drifting past,
The storm of shell has ceased.
Disrupted is the cordon fell,
Sweet charity released.

Forth from the shadow, swift we come
Wrought in the flame together.
All men as one beneath the sun
In brotherhood forever.

RANDOM

QUESTION

Where are the brave men, where are the strong men?
Pygmies rise
And spawn the earth.
Weak-kneed, weak-hearted, and afraid,
Afraid to face the counsel of their timid hearts,
Afraid to look men squarely,
Down they gaze
With fatal fascination
Down, down
Into the whirling maggot sands
Of prejudice.

The Initiate

The woes of flesh are naught
To one who knows
The agony of soul!
'Twere but the thud of wind and rain
Upon the roof.
The woes of flesh are naught
To one who knows!

GEORGIA DOUGLAS JOHNSON

BONDAGE

Many cages round me,
Bar on bar
Stand grim, forbidding!
Ghostly pressures
Clutch my heart.
I gaze with eyes unseeing
Whereunto may I wander free?
Alas, alas!
My garden walks lie inwardly!

RESOLUTION

With but one life full certified,
And that of every gleam denied
My portion,
Close to the unrelenting sod,
E'en as my fathers dumbly trod,
I've slumbered;
But now a surging, wild unrest
Uproots the poppies from my breast,
My soul awake, erect! anew!
I stand and face the star-swept blue,
And swear to make my dreams come true!

GEORGIA DOUGLAS JOHNSON

ECLIPSE

Aflounder the uncompassed darkness of doubt
    In search of the path to the goal
That lies at the end of our transient day,
    The ultimate bourne of the soul;
I grasp into nothingness, feebly essay
    To clasp but a willow, a stone,
And grope through the stepless, unechoing gloom
    Unanswered, unsuccored, 'alone!

WHY

The verdure sleeps in winter,
    Awakes with April rain,
The sun swings low 'tis night ascends,
    And lo! 'tis morn again:
The world spins on triumphant
    Across a trackless sky,
And man seeks evermore in vain
    The primal reason why.

O whither are we rushing?
    And wherefrom were we torn?
We breathe from out the silences,
    And breathless, back are borne.

Deep in the soul are voices
    Returning this reply:
It took a God to make us,
    Only God can answer why!

GEORGIA DOUGLAS JOHNSON

HUSKS

Forever and forevermore,
    Across the heights, the deeps,
Spurred by an ever-flaming zeal
    That slumbers not, nor sleeps
We chase the furtive form of fame
    Beyond the edge of dusk,
To bear within our arms at length,
    An empty mocking, husk!

The Watcher

The long, grim years with iron tread
    Move down the shuttered isle
Of time's unrecking labyrinth
    Paved with forgotten dead.

And I, a feather in their wake,
    Gaze long and tremblingly
Into these sunless corridors,
    Praying the light to break!

The Vanished Road

We're wending the trail of the vanishing road,
With a song and a shout, just to lighten the load,
That lies in the heart, filled with queries and cares,
For never a traveler knows where he fares.

But on with a jest, and rollicksome cheer,
With laughter that leaps, as a veil, for the tear;
The world's weary caravan finds that abode
That lies at the end of the vanishing road.

APPRECIATIONS

SERVICE

When we count out our gold at the end of the day,
And have filtered the dross that has cumbered the way,
Oh, what were the hold of our treasury then
Save the love we have shown to the children of men?

To the Martyred

O sacrificial throng whose lives
Build up the yawning deeps
O'er which we pass reflectively
To broader lights and sweeps.

Know, that we hold with reverence
The signal price you paid,
And all our trophies, one by one,
Upon your bier are laid.

To John Brown

We lift a song to you across the day
Which bears through travailing the seed you spread
In terror's morning, flung with fingers red
In blood of tyrants, who debarred the way
To Freedom's dawning. Hearken to the lay
Chanted by dusky millions, soft and mellow-keyed,
In minor measure, Martyr of the Freed,
A song of memory across the day.

Truth cannot perish though the earth erase
The royal signals, leaving not a trace,
And time still burgeoneth the fertile seed,
Though he is crucified who wrought the deed:
O Alleghanies, fold him to your breast
Until the judgment! Sentinel his rest!

TO ABRAHAM LINCOLN

Within the temple of our heart
Your sacred memory dwells apart,
Where ceaselessly a censor swings
Alight with fragrant offerings;
Nor time, nor tide, nor circumstance
Can dim this grand remembrance,
And all the blood of Afric hue
Beats in one mighty tide for you!

GEORGIA DOUGLAS JOHNSON

To William Stanley Braithwaite

When time has rocked the present age to sleep,
And lighter hearts are lilting to the sway
Of rhythmic poesy's enhanced lay,
Recurring sequences shall fitly keep
Your fame eternal, as they lightly sweep
Aside the curtain to that potent day
When you in primal fervor, led the way
Unto Apollo's narrow winding steep.

None shall forget your travail, utter, sore,
That oped the golden avenue of song,
When, like a knight, so errantly you bore
The mantled children valiantly along,
Their homage as a rising incense sweet
Shall permeate the heavens at your feet!

To W.E.B. Du Bois—Scholar

Grandly isolate as the god of day
Blazing an orbit through the dank and gloom
Of misty morning, far and fair you loom,
Flooding the dimness with your golden ray,
Cheering the mantled on the thorn-set way,
Teaching of Faith and Hope o'er the tomb,
Where both, though buried, spring to newer bloom—
Strengthened and sweet from the mound of decay.

Soft! strains of Sanctus we lift on the air,
Ere Nunc Dimittus at last shall be sung,
Sing we our Sanctus to fitly declare
Blessings that well up from hearts sorely wrung.

Lead, lead us on o'er the furthermost stair
Light of our impotence! Joy of our tongue!

GEORGIA DOUGLAS JOHNSON

To Ridgley Torrence—Playwright

All hail! fair vistas break upon the view,
The gates swing wide and free with clanging sound,
Rejoice! a mighty champion is found,
Son of the morning, prescient and true.
Upon the threshold of a cycle new
He stands, and sentinels its virgin ground,
Seer in his poet-visioning profound,
Presaging vaster reaches skies more blue.

Lifting their misty glances to the day,
The prismic children pass the erstwhile bars,
Exultant, swiftly, boundingly they stray,
Awhile forgetful of deep, hidden scars
Thus, as a golden legend time shall tell
Of him who wrought so mightily and well!

To Richard R. Wright—Instructor

Son of a race, whose dusky visage shows
The heel of fortune, those who walk unfree
Though cradled in the hold of liberty,
Whose shackled spirit every gamut knows
Of Hate's cadenza, through whose warm blood flows
The royal ransom of love's dynasty,
Scion of these, he strides to meet his foes.

Erect, unbending, note his sable brow,
The rugged furrows where deep feelings plough,
The step of vigor and the noble air,
The subtle halo of his wintry hair,
Up from the furnace of the Earth's red sea
A man is fashioned for the years to be!

GEORGIA DOUGLAS JOHNSON

To Samuel Coleridge Taylor, Upon Hearing His

Sometimes I feel like a motherless child

Strange to a sensing motherhood,
Loved as a toy not understood,
Child of a dusky father, bold;
Frail little captive, exiled, cold.

Oft when the brooding planets sleep,
You through their drowsy empires creep,
Flinging your arms through their empty space,
Seeking the breast of an unknown face.

To Emilie Bigelow Hapgood—
Philanthropist

Far from the seried ranks you sway,
    Firm in your own believing
In that frail brotherhood, who stray
    Sore anguishing, sore grieving.
Such hands as yours, adown the years
    Enchain a faith unbroken,
They stay the dreary waste of tears,
    And lift to Hope a token!

GEORGIA DOUGLAS JOHNSON

To Henry Lincoln Johnson—Lawyer

Quite firmly did you stand, and unafraid
Before that haughty bar that sought to hold
You fettered, lest you strengthen and grow bold
To break a clearing through that fetid glade
Which their benighted prejudice—had made;
They taunted you with darkling hints of gold,
Preferring you were bought as you had sold,
They weaved their webs like spiders in the shade.

But as a giant in the falling night
Of storm, you forged afore with ruthless tread,
To offer up your heart's blood in the fight,
Forgetting self, unmindful, unafraid,
Nor pausing until thrice acclaimed the right
To rally in the tents of those you led.

To Mary Church Terrell—Lecturer

A pioneer, she blazed a trail of light
Through murky shadows, with a lithesome tread
Unto those forums, where Hope's beams are shed:
Straight through the mighty cordon of the night,
Rapt with a vision, soul-born, clear and bright,
Leaving the South of frigid wrong, she sped
Into the North, where hearts glow warm instead,
A people's tragedy to there recite.

Hope's liquid pipings lift their tender lay,
Morning is waking, flushed with rosy gleam,
Night with its shadow winds with yesterday
Adown the world-way as an inky stream,
Seed time and harvest deftly interplay,
And Life's fruition is its vital dream!

GEORGIA DOUGLAS JOHNSON

To May Howard Jackson—Sculptor

You saw the vision in the face of clay,
And fixed it through the magic of a hand
Obedient unto the will's command,
In forms impervious to Time's decay:
Historian of bloods that interplay
Confusedly within a cryptic land,
You've chiseled, and your work of art shall stand
To gem the archives of a better day.

Alone, far from the touch of kindred mind,
You've mounted with a grim, determined zeal,
Despite environment austere, unkind,
Or frozen-fingers clenched to your appeal,
You've held the ardor of your first ideal,
Robed in a queenly majesty, resigned.

To The Memory of Inez Milholland

Folded in silent veils of sleep,
    You calmly rest,
For God hath spoken, should we weep?
    He knoweth best.

But rather let us garner still
    While yet we may,
And meet you in His Holy Hill
    On that Great Day!

GEORGIA DOUGLAS JOHNSON

To Atlanta University—Its Founders and Teachers

Pass down the aisle of buried years tonight,
And stand uncovered in that holy place
Where noble structures lift their hallowed height
Beneath a bending Heaven's chaste embrace,
The fruit of those who scorned the path of ease,
To buckle on the armaments of care
Like to the Son of Man Himself, were these
Who gave themselves for brother men less fair.

Before the blinding footlights of today
We man our parts within Life's tragic play,
Full mindful of the earnest love and care
That keeps eternal watch and vigil there;
Nor do they need fair monuments and scrolls
Their memories are deathless in our souls.

A Note About the Author

Georgia Douglas Johnson (1880–1966) was an African American poet and playwright. Born in Atlanta, she excelled in school from a young age, learning to read, write, and play violin. She graduated from Atlanta University's Normal School in 1896 before working briefly as a teacher Marietta, Georgia. In 1902, having decided to become a professional musician, she enrolled at Oberlin Conservatory of Music, where she studied music theory and learned the art of composition. She later returned to Atlanta, marrying prominent lawyer and Republican party member Henry Lincoln Johnson, with whom she had two sons. After moving to Washington, D.C. in 1910, she embarked on a literary career against her husband's wishes, submitting poems to journals around the country. She published her first collection, *The Heart of a Woman and Other Poems* (1918) to modest acclaim and continued to grow her reputation with poems in *The Crisis*, the journal of the NAACP edited by W.E.B. Du Bois. Following her husband's death in 1925, she supported herself and her sons with various jobs and maintained a staggering output of poems, plays, short stories, and newspaper columns. She also began hosting prominent figures of the Harlem Renaissance at her home, which she called the S Street Salon, providing a meeting place for such legendary artists and intellectuals as Langston Hughes, Jean Toomer, Alain Locke, and Eulalie Spence. She is recognized today as a prominent anti-lynching activist, a pioneering poet, and one of the first African American woman playwrights.

A Note from the Publisher

bookfinity & **MINT EDITIONS**

Enjoy more of your favorite classics with Bookfinity,
a new search and discovery experience for readers.
With Bookfinity, you can discover more vintage
literature for your collection, find your Reader Type,
track books you've read or want to read,
and add reviews to your favorite books.
Visit www.bookfinity.com, and click on
Take the Quiz to get started.

Don't forget to follow us
@bookfinityofficial and @mint_editions

CPSIA information can be obtained
at www.ICGtesting.com
Printed in the USA
BVHW061551261222
654959BV00003B/261

9 781513 209241